First Facts™

Our Government

The State
Judicial Branch

by Mary Firestone

Consultant:
National Center for State Courts
Williamsburg, Virginia

Capstone
press

Mankato, Minnesota

First Facts is published by Capstone Press
151 Good Counsel Drive, P.O. Box 669, Mankato, Minnesota 56002
http://www.capstonepress.com

Library of Congress Cataloging-in-Publication Data
Firestone, Mary.
    The State judicial branch/by Mary Firestone.
    p. cm.—(First facts. Our government)
    Summary: Introduces state supreme courts, including how their justices are selected,
how they operate, and how cases are decided.
    Includes bibliographical references and index.
    ISBN 0-7368-2503-7 (hardcover)
    1. Courts of last resort—United States—States—Juvenile literature. [1. Courts of last
resort—United States—States. 2. Courts.] I. Title. II. Series.
KF8736.Z9F57 2004
347.73'26—dc22   2003012138

Editorial Credits
Christine Peterson, editor; Jennifer Bergstrom, designer; Jo Miller, photo researcher;
    Eric Kudalis, product planning editor

Photo Credits
AP/Wide World Photos/Lauren McFalls, 7; Paul Sakuma, 8–9; Ruby Washington, 13;
    Steve Pope, 14–15; Wade Payne, 17
Corbis/James Marshall, 5; Reuters NewMedia Inc., 12
Getty Images Inc./AFP, cover; Newsmakers, 11, 18–19
North Wind Picture Archives, 20

1 2 3 4 5 6 09 08 07 06 05 04

Table of Contents

State Courts Make Rulings

The state judicial branch decides **cases** and makes **rulings** on laws. Many state courts study laws on education. Most kids go to a school. Some parents teach their kids at home. State high courts ruled parents must follow state laws when teaching kids at home.

 Fun Fact:
In the United States, there are about 15,000 courts.

State Government

Parts of state government have different jobs. The legislative branch writes and passes bills. The executive branch makes sure laws are followed.

Parts of State Government

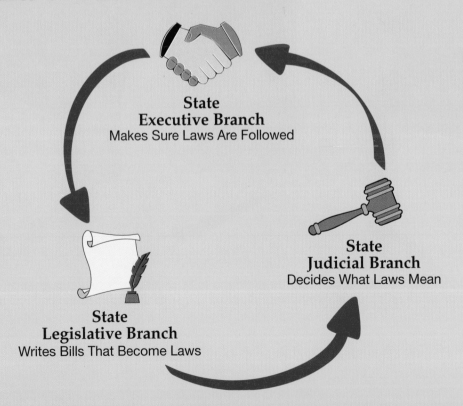

State Executive Branch
Makes Sure Laws Are Followed

State Judicial Branch
Decides What Laws Mean

State Legislative Branch
Writes Bills That Become Laws

The judicial branch decides what laws mean. Courts also deal with people who break laws. The highest state court is often called a supreme court.

Justices Serve the Court

Justices serve on each state's highest court. High courts have five, seven, or nine justices. In some states, people vote for justices. In other states, **governors** and lawmakers choose justices. Some justices serve for six to 14 years. Others may serve until they **retire**.

 Fun Fact:
State high courts have an odd number of justices so there cannot be tie votes on rulings.

9

Chief Justices

A chief justice leads the highest court in each state. These leaders are the first to talk at court meetings. Chief justices from every state meet each year. Together, they talk about how to make sure court rulings are fair.

Justices Study Cases

People ask high courts to hear many cases each year. Justices look over rulings. They choose cases to hear in court.

Most high court cases are about state laws. Justices use state laws to make their rulings. They also study rulings from lower courts.

Justices Are Busy People

Justices do many things. They meet with court workers. They visit other courts in their state. Justices hear cases in court. They write reports called **opinions** to explain their rulings.

 Fun Fact:
In many states, justices hear cases in more than one city so more people can see how the court works.

High Courts Hear Appeals

The highest court in each state hears **appeals**. Appeals are cases that were decided by lower courts. People may not like a ruling. They can ask a higher court to study the case. The higher court may not agree to hear the case. People then must follow the lower court ruling.

 Fun Fact:
In most states, justices must first be lawyers in order to serve on a high court.

Justices Decide

Justices decide cases in the states' highest courts. **Lawyers** tell justices about a case. Justices then ask questions. They meet to talk about the case. Justices then vote on a ruling to decide the case.

Fun Fact:
The first case heard by the Minnesota Supreme Court was about a stray cow. A man wanted $2 because a cow wandered onto his land.

Amazing But True!

In the 1800s, many state court justices rode horses to court. Justices traveled many miles (kilometers) to hear cases in small towns. Lawyers and other people sometimes went with the justice. Court was often held in people's homes. Justices often were gone for many weeks. They carried law books, clothes, and supplies with them.

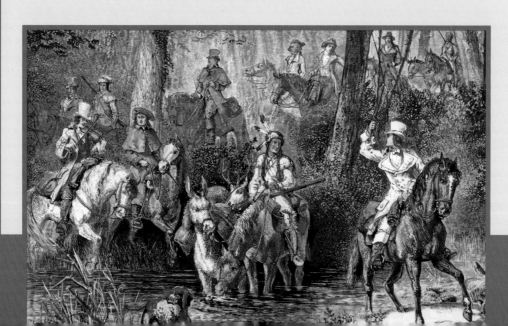

Hands On: Be A Justice

State court justices make rulings after they listen to the facts about a case. Pretend you are a justice and decide the case of *Goldilocks and the Three Bears*.

What You Need

a copy of *Goldilocks and the Three Bears*
an adult
paper
pencil

What You Do

1. Get a copy of the story *Goldilocks and the Three Bears* from your school or local library.
2. If needed, have an adult read the story to you.
3. Talk about the story. Did Goldilocks break any laws?
4. Be a justice and decide the case.
5. If you think Goldilocks broke the law, decide what should happen next. What can Goldilocks do to help the bears? How can she make up for the trouble she caused the bears? Write your ideas down in a ruling.
6. If you decide Goldilocks did not break any laws, write down why you made that decision.

Glossary

appeal (uh-PEEL)—to ask a higher court to review a case already decided by a lower court

case (KAYSS)—a legal problem settled in court

governor (GUHV-urn-or)—the leader of a state's executive branch of government

justice (JUHSS-tiss)—a member of a state's highest court

lawyer (LAW-yur)—a person who is trained to advise people about the law; lawyers act and speak for people in court.

opinion (uh-PIN-yuhn)—a report by a judge or jury giving the legal reasons for a court's ruling

retire (ri-TIRE)—to give up work usually because of a person's age

ruling (ROO-ling)—a decision made by a court

Read More

Dubois, Muriel L. *The U.S. Supreme Court*. First Facts: Our Government. Mankato, Minn.: Capstone Press, 2004.

Giesecke, Ernestine. *State Government*. Kids' Guide. Chicago: Heinemann Library, 2000.

Internet Sites

FactHound offers a safe, fun way to find Internet sites related to this book. All of the sites on FactHound have been researched by our staff.

Here's how:
1) Visit *www.facthound.com*
2) Type in this special code **0736825037** for age-appropriate sites. Or enter a search word related to this book for a more general search.
3) Click on the Fetch It button.

FactHound will fetch the best sites for you!

Index